"A truly brilliant concept that allows you to see returns we love AND make an impact for God's glory around the world!!"
– David & Jason Benham, Best-Selling Authors, Entrepreneurs

INVESTING WITH PURPOSE

Real Estate Investment that Allows You to Increase Your Profits While Impacting Lives

STEVEN LIBMAN

Copyright © 2024, Integrity Holdings Group.
All rights reserved.

No part of this book may be reproduced or transmitted in any form or by any means, electronic or mechanical, including photocopying, recording, or by any information retrieval system, without permission in writing from the publisher.

Publishing Process by www.PlugAndPlayPublishing.com
Book Cover by Tracey Miller | www.TraceOfStyle.com
Book Edited by Jenny Butterfield Lyon and Becky Shipkosky

EARNINGS & INCOME DISCLAIMER: This book contains statements that are forward-looking within the meaning of the Private Securities Litigation Reform Act of 1995. These include statements regarding Integrity Holdings Group and the Integrity Holdings Group Opportunity Fund, talking about our future growth, momentum, operations, market share, business outlook, and financial performance expectations. These statements are estimates only, and actual results may ultimately differ from them. Except to the extent required by applicable security laws, we undertake no obligation to update or revise any of the forward-looking statements that you may read in this book.

The purchaser and/or reader of these materials assumes all responsibility for the use of this information. Steven Libman, Integrity Holdings Group, and Publisher assume no responsibility and/or liability whatsoever for any purchaser and/or reader of these materials.

In addition, with respect to the reliability, accuracy, timeliness, usefulness, adequacy, completeness, and/or suitability of information provided in this book, Steven Libman, Integrity Holdings Group, its partners, associates, affiliates, consultants, and/or presenters make no warranties, guarantees, representations, or claims of any kind. Readers' results will vary depending on a number of factors. Any and all claims or representations as to income earnings are not to be considered as average earnings. Testimonials are not representative. This book and all products and services are for educational and informational purposes only. Use caution and see the advice of qualified professionals. Check with your accountant, attorney, or professional advisor before acting on this or any information. You agree that Steven Libman and/or Integrity Holdings Group is not responsible for the success or failure of your personal, business, health, or financial decisions relating to any information presented by Steven Libman, Integrity Holdings Group, or company products/services. Earnings potential is entirely dependent on the efforts, skills, and application of the individual person. Any examples, stories, references, or case studies are for illustrative purposes only and should not be interpreted as testimonies and/or examples of what reader and/or consumers can generally expect from the information. No representation in any part of this information, materials and/or seminar training are guarantees or promises for actual performance. Any statements, strategies, concepts, techniques, exercises and ideas in the information, materials and/or seminar training offered are simply opinion or experience and thus should not be misinterpreted as promises, typical results or guarantees (expressed or implied). The author and publisher (Steven Libman, Integrity Holdings Group, or any of Integrity Holdings Group's representatives) shall in no way, under any circumstances, be held liable to any party (or third party) for any direct, indirect, punitive, special, incidental or other consequential damages arising directly or indirectly from any use of books, materials, and/or seminar trainings, which is provided "as is," and without warranties.

To my beloved wife, Grace.
You've been my unwavering supporter in business and in life. Your endless encouragement and steadfast belief in me, even when I didn't believe in myself and our pockets were empty, have been my guiding light. Your grace and strength have carried us through every challenge, and I'm forever grateful for your love and unwavering faith.
Grace^2. All my love. All my life.

To my dear children, Cadence, Harper, and Noah.
As you embark on your journey through life, I dedicate this book, *Investing with Purpose*, to you. May its principles guide you in the intersection of faith and finance, teaching you the importance of biblical stewardship and the true value of money. Remember, my dear ones, never to buy into the world's lie that you are not smart enough to manage your own finances. With God's wisdom and guidance, you are capable of achieving greatness.

"'For I know the plans I have for you,' declares the Lord,
'plans to prosper you and not to harm you,
plans to give you hope and a future.'"
- Jeremiah 29:11 (NIV)

With all my love,
Steven (Dad)

Table of Contents

Author's Note 1

Read This First 5

Chapter 1 7
Achieving Financial Independence Through Real Estate

Chapter 2 17
Align Your Investments with Your Core Values

Chapter 3 33
Stand Out from the Crowd

Chapter 4 39
Shoot for the Big Three

Chapter 5 49
Establish Your Mission Money Matrix

Chapter 6 61
Invest with Purpose

Chapter 7 69
Invest for Impact

Chapter 8 85
Frequently Asked Questions

Your Next Steps 95

About the Author 97

About Integrity Holdings Group 99

Motivate and Inspire Others! 101

Are You Looking for a Faith-Based Speaker? 103

Acknowledgements 105

Author's Note

Before we get started, there are two important things I need to cover for you. First, this book is titled *Investing with Purpose*, and it shares the same name as our online brand at InvestingWithPurpose.org. However, the name of our company is Integrity Holdings Group. I don't want to confuse you, so please note that inside this book, we'll be using these names interchangeably.

Investing with Purpose, InvestingWithPurpose.org, and Integrity Holdings Group all mean the same thing. They are all part of our brand.

Second, since this is a book about real estate investing, it's important that you see and understand our legal disclaimer. In short, this book contains statements that are forward-looking within the meaning of the Private Securities Litigation Reform Act of 1995. These include statements regarding Integrity Holdings Group and the Integrity Holdings Group Opportunity Fund, talking about our future growth, momentum, operations, market share, business outlook, and financial performance expectations. These statements are estimates only and actual results may ultimately differ from them. Except to the extent required by applicable security laws, we undertake no obligation to update or revise any of the forward-looking statements that you may read in this book.

For our full disclaimer, please visit:
InvestingWithPurpose.org/disclaimer

With all this out of the way, congratulations on picking up this book! I hope you enjoy the material inside as much as I enjoyed writing it for you!

- Steven Libman
Co-Founder and Managing Partner
at Integrity Holdings Group
InvestingWithPurpose.org

"You are endowed by your Creator with the right to pursue freedom and happiness."

Read This First

The Declaration of Independence states, "We hold these truths to be self-evident, that all men are created equal, that they are endowed by their Creator with certain unalienable rights, that among these are Life, Liberty, and the pursuit of Happiness."

Read that again. You are endowed by your Creator with the right to pursue freedom and happiness.

In other words, you have a God-given right to pursue the life of your choosing. To do what you want, when you want, with whom you want. But to have that kind of freedom, you must have a certain level of financial independence.

Now, I know some Christians might be resistant to the idea of achieving financial freedom like this because there is an idea in the Christian community that you need to be poor to be a good Christian. "Money is the root of all evil," right? Achieving too much wealth might lead to being too prideful, too greedy, or too selfish. As Christians, isn't that what the majority of us have been taught?

In truth, money is not the root of all evil. It's the *love* of money that's the root of all evil. It's when you love money more than you love God, your wife, or your kids. It's when you love money more than you love your family or friends. It's when you love money so much that you let greed get the better of you. It's when you *love* money, not when you *have* money.

Money is not the root of all evil. Money is simply a tool to get you and your family what you need and want. And it's a tool that can help others get what they need and want.

With money, we have more options. Without money, we have very limited options. With money, we can focus on loving people, helping people, and giving to people. Without money, we have to resort to living in survival mode and actively work from paycheck to paycheck.

Money is simply a tool. And with enough money, we can be a force for good and a force for God!

That's why, in this book, I'd like to introduce you to the idea that achieving wealth and financial freedom can also help you fulfill your Christian mission on Earth.

Are you ready to get started?

Let's start by looking at how you can achieve financial independence through real estate!

Chapter 1
Achieving Financial Independence Through Real Estate

In our first chapter together, I want to take the time to define "financial freedom" for you and talk a little bit more about why you should care about your financial independence. Then, I want to give you some practical advice about how to reach financial freedom through real estate investing.

So, what is financial freedom? To me, financial freedom means I have enough money that I no longer need a job and get to do whatever I want with my time. It means I get to wake up in the morning and know that all my monthly bills are taken care of and paid for and that I can do what I want when I want with whomever I want. And it means I no longer have to ask permission to do what I would like to do that day.

Can you imagine having that kind of peace of mind? Imagine knowing that even if you got sick or (God forbid) were in some kind of accident, your bills and your family were going to be taken care of no matter what.

That's the kind of financial independence that I'm talking about. The kind that leads to ultimate emotional and spiritual freedom in your life. The freedom to pursue what God is calling you to do, without having to worry about money.

And that's why you should care about achieving financial independence for yourself and for your family. So that all your bills are taken care of. So that you're able to live comfortably without being required to work at any kind of job. And so that you have the ultimate freedom to bless others and make a real impact both in your local community and in the world at large.

I'm getting a little bit ahead of myself here.

Before we start talking about how you can use your blessings to bless others, I want you to know that the reason my wife and I got into real estate investing is because, throughout history, the majority of millionaires in this country were made through their real estate investments. And I've discovered no faster way to achieve financial freedom than by investing in real estate deals.

With that in mind, let me show you how to…

Achieve Financial Freedom Through Real Estate Investing

Let's talk on a very practical, real-world level about how real estate investing can change your life.

In short, real estate investing leads to passive income, and passive income leads to financial independence. First, let me go a little more in-depth to explain what passive income is, then I'll tell you how investing in real estate can help you create passive income that will have a real impact on your family.

There are two types of income: active and passive.

Active income is when you're trading time for dollars. You get a W-2 or a 1099 at tax time. Or if you're an entrepreneur and haven't set up a business that earns you passive income, then you have to be active in the day-to-day operation of your business. Even then, you still have a job. The bottom line is you don't have passive income. You're working for every single dollar that comes to your family.

But the key to financial freedom is passive income. And so, what is passive income, and why do you care? Why are you working to get to a place of passive income only? If you are seeking financial freedom, meaning that at the end of the day you can pay your bills without having to go and trade time for money, you need passive income. Simply put, passive income is regular cash flow that you don't need to work for. Your money does the work for you.

To get started, if you truly want real financial independence, you need to know what *your number* is.

Go through your last six months of bank statements and see what your expenses have been. Take those expenses, add 10 or 15% as a buffer, and then that number is approximately what you need to make in passive income so that you can quit your job, sell your business, or otherwise exit the rat race. That number will give you the opportunity to say, "I am financially free. The money that I have coming in passively outweighs my expenses. I don't have to go trade time for money anymore."

To me, that's what financial freedom means. If you don't have to punch a clock and you don't have to go do stuff for work, then you get to spend the time with your family that you want to. You get to volunteer when and where you want to. You can work on your health. You can wake up and work out and pray and meditate in the mornings. You can spend time with your kids. Having that passive income gives you that freedom. That's the kind of financial freedom that we're talking about.

And so, how do you generate passive income and achieve financial freedom? There are so many ways to make passive income. You can flip houses, you can write a book, or you can create an online course and sell it. You can design products online. There are a multitude of things to do that require less and less time, but I don't know of a single one that takes less time to generate passive income than real estate investing.

One of the things that always drew me to real estate was knowing that more millionaires were made through real estate investing than any other path. To invest in real estate, you don't need to know how to write. You don't need to know how to design websites. You don't know how to create products and sell them. You don't need to go out and raise capital. With real estate investing, you just need a little bit of capital and a little bit of research. You can invest in real estate and build multiple streams of passive income, one deal at a time.

An extra $1000 or $2000 a month starts to relieve a lot of financial pressure. If your mortgage is $1800 a month and you can get into a deal that's going to be producing $1800 a month, then you've just replaced your mortgage cost. You could do that for every single expense that you have until you reach your freedom number.

Once you start finding opportunities and investing in deals, track your progress. As you're building every stream of income, keep track of where you are in your goal to create passive income. Every deal is different, but you can figure out what each investment is going to produce for you in terms of passive income. Then, you will start to get a picture of what you're going to make over five years, ten years, etc.

> **BONUS STEP**
>
> If you want to reach that freedom number faster, tighten your belt. Figure out a way to decrease some of your expenses. If you go through your analysis of six months' worth of expenses and you figure out that they're $10,000 a month, perhaps you can take steps to reduce your bills and spending. If you decide you really only need $8,000 a month to live comfortably, you can reach your freedom number that much faster.

Get a few of those deals going, with your freedom number as your income goal, and you'll build your passive income brick-by-brick.

Your passive income increases over time. Then, you can start to figure out, "Hey, by this date, I'm going to be financially free, and I'll be able to quit my job if I choose to do so." If you don't want to quit your job, that's fine. Your choice. But you might want to go part-time. You might want to stack more cash. You may want to enable your spouse to retire early. When you get to this point in the financial freedom journey, you have options to choose from!

Every passive stream of income that you add covers more and more living expenses. Then sooner or later, you get to the tipping point where you feel comfortable reducing your number of work hours or quitting your job altogether. You get to start deciding what you want to do and when you want to do it.

The steps that I'm outlining in this book are going to help you identify your personal and passive income goals, create a path towards investing that generates passive income, and track your progress.

No matter what your reasons are for wanting to build passive income, follow these steps. You'll get to a place of financial assurance, and you'll be able to quit your job with confidence. You can only do that if you have money coming in because money is a necessary tool. Once you're no longer trading your time for dollars, that passive income will change the entire dynamic of your life.

Reach out to us at InvestingWithPurpose.org if you want some more in-depth help and analysis. We offer guidance about how to find your freedom number and guidance about how to track your progress in your journey toward financial freedom.

If you're already invested in real estate, you're already starting to see some of the benefits that passive income offers. We have a couple of investors that talk to us all the time about the fact that they take off whenever they want and go travel the world with their kids, which is an incredible opportunity.

And then we have people who are just starting out with us who are trying to dig their way out of some student loan debt or credit card debt, trying to buy a house, and starting to plan for the future. My wife and I started there too. We all start somewhere. As Vince Lombardi famously said, "The man on top of the mountain didn't fall there."

Now that my wife and I are further along in our real estate investing, we're doing larger acquisitions, getting more cash flow, and achieving our financial independence. And we're so grateful that we chose to take that first step of buying our first piece of real estate.

I hope that this chapter has started to give you a taste of what's possible through real estate investing. And I hope that you're starting to get excited about how your life can drastically change by creating multiple streams of passive income.

In the next chapter, I'm going to show you how real estate investing can lead to not only financial freedom but personal fulfillment as well. I can't emphasize enough that investing in real estate is spiritual. The scripture mentions real estate in multiple places where God encourages us and promises us land.

One of these scriptures that I revisit often is Deuteronomy 1:8 (NIV), "See, I have given you this land. Go in and take possession of the land the Lord swore he would give to your fathers—to Abraham, Isaac, and Jacob—and to their descendants after them."

Our journey together is just getting started.

"The key to financial freedom is passive income."

Chapter 2
Align Your Investments with Your Core Values

There's financial freedom, and then there's spiritual freedom. When those things are aligned, that's how you find true fulfillment. And at the end of the day, you're reading this book because you want to see dollars coming into your bank account without having to go to work. That's great, but ultimately what's behind that desire? The 'why' behind the 'why' behind the 'why' is you want fulfillment, right? You want to be satisfied. There's something more that is ultimately kind of missing or there's a gaping hole. And I'm going to tell you, I'm here to help you put words to that empty feeling you might have.

If you struggle with really understanding how to use your gifts, the talents that you've been given, and steward them well, this chapter is just for you. I want to teach you how to connect the values that you want to cultivate and incorporate those values into your finances and your investing.

In this chapter, I am going to cover three main points to help you find more fulfillment with your investing and reach for both types of freedom (financial and spiritual) at the same time. First, I'm going to help you define your core values. Second, I'm going to show you how to steward those good gifts that you've been given. And third, I'm going to teach you how to connect your investment plan to your spiritual life.

I think that says it all. Let's get started.

Defining Your Core Values

As you may have already guessed, I'm a follower of Christ and the call of Christianity. With that call in mind, it may be easier for you to envision how to live and give with purpose.

When I first started down this path of incorporating Christ into my business, I hired a business coach who told me to write a mission statement and come up with a list of core values to help drive my decisions. So, I did just that.

I wrote a company mission statement. And I wrote a family mission statement. And from there, I wrote two lists of core values, one for my business and one for my family. And you may or may not be surprised to learn that both sets of documents are very closely aligned. By getting clear on your core values and understanding why you do what you do, you'll be able to easily find opportunities that fit into those core values.

This is a great exercise to do with your spouse or your business partner (if you have one). You can sit down and identify some things that you value. Just start the conversation, and don't be afraid to go deep.

Here's how to really dig into this process and start narrowing down your core values:

1. Think of people in your life whom you respect or look up to. Or maybe think about historical figures you admire. Who are people that are just superheroes to you?
2. Write down some of the qualities that you love or respect about those people.
3. Pick two, three, or four people, and then write down some of their qualities that you admire and want in your life too.

What's interesting about coming up with core values this way is you don't see what you like in other people because you long to have that quality. I believe it's because God already placed that quality within you. I believe that you admire those people because they are like mirrors for you, so what you're recognizing is the embodiment of what is already inside of you.

For example, I teach an entrepreneurship class at a homeschool co-op. And when I do this exercise with the students, all these kids sit around and voice their favorite qualities about their parents. I have 14-year-old kids saying, "My mom is strong-willed. My dad is really brave and honoring. Honest." What I want you to realize is that they named qualities their parents are already teaching them or passing on to them. By naming these qualities in others, we can claim these qualities for ourselves.

So, that's the easy way to start this exercise.

Go through your list and see where the overlap is. There are probably qualities that you wrote down more than once. Those are the qualities and values that are really hitting home. Those are the attributes that will become your core values.

BONUS STEP

I would encourage you to look at the people on your list and send a letter to each of them. "Dear So-and-So, I just want to let you know I was coming up with my core values, and such-and-such quality of yours really rang true for me. I respect this about you." It'll bless them, and it'll be a fun end to the exercise. Give it a try!

For my family core values, I simply sat down with my wife, and we came up with a list that we both agreed on.

The process for my business was a little bit more involved.

As the leader or visionary, you need to make the final call about what goes on the list for your business, but everybody should be involved in coming up with the list. At my company, we all sat around in a room together to generate our list. We got input from everybody.

For example, our first core value is Christ-centeredness, and we understand that we're not going to only hire Christians, but you need to act in accordance with Christ-like values. So, if you're outside of Christ's likeness in terms of integrity or honor, then that's where you would violate this core value.

Then, we added respect to the list. Everybody deserves respect. We continued through this process until we had a list of five core values for the company. By going through this exercise with your whole team, you can create a list that everyone agrees to, is aware of, and agrees to follow.

Beyond simply making everyone at the company aware, setting the list of core values together sets the expectation of behavior at your company. Now that we're all in agreement that these are our values, let's act accordingly. I think frustration is born out of expectations not meeting up with reality. So, even though we can't control reality, setting expectations is the thing that we can control.

Putting both lists together is an excellent baseline for setting expectations with everybody and getting everyone on the same page. And those are the core tenets that you should look to when making decisions about your life and your investments.

Are You Being a Good Steward of Your Gifts?

The next step is to look at your life, your decisions, your time, and your investments and ask yourself if your life aligns with these core tenets.

Have you ever stopped and thought about why there seems to be some sort of friction in your life?

I am going to just throw this out there. As a believer, you may be living parts of your life that are not necessarily fully aligned with your core values.

The Parable of the Talents is one of my favorite stories from the Bible. Let's review it here.

The Parable of Talents

[14] For it will be like a man going on a journey, who called his servants [a] and entrusted to them his property. [15] To one he gave five talents, [b] to another two, to another one, to each according to his ability. Then he went away. [16] He who had received the five talents went at once and traded

with them, and he made five talents more. [17] So also, he who had the two talents made two talents more. [18] But he who had received the one talent went and dug in the ground and hid his master's money. [19] Now after a long time, the master of those servants came and settled accounts with them. [20] And he who had received the five talents came forward, bringing five talents more, saying, 'Master, you delivered to me five talents; here, I have made five talents more.' [21] His master said to him, 'Well done, good and faithful servant. [c] You have been faithful over a little; I will set you over much. Enter into the joy of your master.' [22] And he also who had the two talents came forward, saying, 'Master, you delivered to me two talents; here, I have made two talents more.' [23] His master said to him, 'Well done, good and faithful servant. You have been faithful over a little; I will set you over much. Enter into the joy of your master.' [24] He also who had received the one talent came forward, saying, 'Master, I knew you to be a hard man, reaping where you did not sow, and gathering where you scattered no seed, [25] so I was afraid, and I went and hid your talent in the ground. Here, you have what is yours.' [26] But his master answered him, 'You wicked and slothful servant! You knew that I reap where I have not sown and gather where I scattered no seed? [27] Then you ought to have invested my money with the bankers, and at my coming, I should have received what was my own with interest.' [28] So take the talent from him and give it to him who has the ten talents. [29] For to everyone who has will more be given, and he will have an abundance. But from the one who has not, even what he has will be taken away. [30] And cast the worthless servant into the outer darkness. In that place, there will be weeping and gnashing of teeth.

Source: Matthew 25:14-30. Life Church/YouVersion, 2016, https://www.bible.com/bible/59/MAT.25.14-30.ESV
The ESV Bible.

Stewardship is important to God, or in this parable, the master. And I think we need to understand that when we're given resources, it's our responsibility to steward those resources well, and it's our responsibility to multiply those resources. Not just add to the resources but multiply them.

So, now that you've defined your core values, how are you going to steward your resources in accordance with those values?

In what ways can you be generous? The Lord loves a cheerful giver, so how can you continue to give more abundantly and more abundantly and more abundantly?

Well, first you have to multiply resources if you're going to be able to become a cheerful giver. The more money you make, the more you can give, and the more impact that you can make on the world around you. Personally, I know that I wasn't called to go be a missionary on the front lines or digging wells in Africa. But God gave me the gift of business and stewardship in the way that we can go and write checks for the people who are on the front lines and digging the wells.

Whenever you make a decision about where you're going to spend money, try to be aware of whether or not spending the money is in alignment with your values. Ask yourself, "Hey, does this go with or against my Christian worldview?" Just be mindful of it.

When you make a decision to invest in something, is that investment aligned with your core values? And will that investment give you the best rate of return on your capital so that you can continue to multiply your resources and fund more core-value-driven things?

Here at InvestingWithPurpose.org, we steward not just our investors' money, but we steward our tenants as well. We have over 980 families living on one property. So overall, we're stewarding thousands of families around the country.

Both locally where our tenants live and nationally across our entire portfolio of properties, we work hard to create culture and community. We love on people.

When a single mom comes home from the hospital with a baby, our property manager will go drop off diapers, wipes, and maybe a $25 laundry gift card. The first couple of weeks of transition as a single mom can be brutal, and we want them to feel cared for and less alone.

We also do movies under the stars so that families can gather and watch a movie in the courtyard.

These little things add up to create a community that aligns with our core values and serves the tenants.

So, take a moment to ask yourself, "Are you stewarding your resources according to your core values? And are you using your core values to guide your financial decisions?" Becoming an effective steward and aligning your investments with your core values can be easier than you think.

The Impact of Aligning Your Investments with Your Core Values

When I realized I could reach for financial freedom and spiritual freedom at the same time by aligning my investments with my core values, it was an "aha!" moment for me. I could do both! I could leave a legacy for my kids *and* build an eternal legacy in heaven by funding nonprofits around the world. And you can do the very same thing.

Shifting my focus and aligning Integrity Holdings Group with my core values allowed my company to grow while giving back in a very real way.

That first year we began to focus on our Christian values, we gave away something like $2500. Last year, we funded over 28 different nonprofits around the world and impacted over 250,000 lives through that giving. And every time I say the number "250,000," I feel like I almost get lost in how impactful it is.

That number includes feeding 15,000 Nicaraguan children, whom we feed every single day and otherwise would not get to eat. That number includes 400 Afghani refugees whom we were able to help escape Afghanistan during the U.S. withdrawal by buying the fuel to refuel the jet planes and fly them to safety. That number includes purchasing vans to rescue over 100 Ukrainians a day from the warzone during the Russian invasion. That number includes 15 Ukrainian girls who we helped save from being trafficked by funding a special-forces rescue mission.

We are grateful to be a small part of these stories.

The famous missionary, William Carey, once said, "I will go down into the pit, if you will hold the rope." You may not be called to go to the front lines of these situations, but you can hold the ropes!

That's the real impact.

Start listening to some of the stories of what nonprofits have been able to do with the generosity of their donors. And man, I hope it fires you up!

I use these stories to get my team pumped up. I mean, we are always looking at the reports and analyzing deals. But I always analyze the deal to maximize the profit so that not only do our investors make the best return they can, but we can give that more to these organizations that need a lot of help.

There's no shortage of need in the world. These organizations are doing really good work. I'm always asking myself, "How do we fund that work?"

It's such an important thing to start thinking through if your investments are impacting the world in the way you want them to.

This question of alignment comes up a lot with Wall Street investors who come to us and want to start considering alternative assets and alternative investments like real estate.

Let me share an example with you.

I had a conversation with a woman who was a retired pastor, and all of her money was in a 401k. We went through her investment portfolio, and I asked, "Do you know what you're invested in?"

She answered, "Yeah, I'm in the Vanguard 100 fund."

I had been down this road before, and I knew exactly where this conversation was headed.

She could see my skepticism, and she continued, "It's returning really well."

I asked her, "Do you want to know what companies are in the Vanguard 100 fund?"

She responded, "Sure." So, we looked up the Vanguard 100 up and went through all the companies that were part of the fund. Lo and behold, the top 30 holdings were all companies that I would argue are antithetical to her worldview. Meaning they promoted political agendas, funded political parties, or funded agendas that were not aligned with her faith.

She had no idea. She almost fell out of her chair.

Your financial adviser is not going to tell you that your money is invested in companies that go against your faith. He's not going to say, "Hey, what are your core values? And let's make sure that the companies we're investing in align with those values." That's not his job.

So, I think a lot of "aha!" moments come from digging in and recognizing you can't un-ring the bell, but you can do better moving forward.

Once you see how to better align with your values, it just depends on how committed you want to be. Are your purchases and your investments aligning with what's important to you? There are alternative investments out there that can align with your values *and* get you a return on your investment. You don't have to choose between the two to grow your wealth and make a difference in the world.

Kingdom Impact

Now that you've defined your core values and started to think more critically about how to align your investments with those values, let's look at how you can make an impact and change lives.

Practically speaking, it's a good idea to get involved with local organizations. Your check won't get lost in the mail, and you'll be able to see right away if the organization's work aligns with your values.

At Integrity Holdings Group, we interview new nonprofits every single quarter. We have a quarterly board meeting. We go through the new nonprofits that we're vetting and make sure that their core values align with our core values. Deciding which organizations to support is a difficult thing sometimes. Again, there's no shortage of need.

But the first step in making an impact is always defining the core values. The heart of the problem is that you deserve to get a spiritual return on investment the same way you get a financial return on investment. And the two are aligned much more closely than you would imagine.

"The more money you make, the more you can give, and the more impact that you can make on the world around you."

At every one of our properties, we give an apartment away (rent-free) to an onsite minister through a local nonprofit. Some people sneer at that idea, thinking that we must be making money hand over fist to do that. Others think that we're being foolish and giving away too much profit.

But in reality, this arrangement is both Biblical and practical.

By giving away the apartment, we're fulfilling our dedication to one of our core tenets of adhering to our Christian values. And we're helping to create the community of love that's so important to us.

From a practical standpoint, since everyone in the community we create sees and appreciates the culture of love, lease turnover is reduced by over 40% at all of those properties. People don't leave, which has a huge impact on our bottom line and your return on investment!

So, don't give in to the idea that you need to choose between financial freedom and spiritual freedom. It is Biblical to make money, be a good steward of your wealth, and create impact in the world. You can have both. And I'm here to teach you how.

Chapter 3
Stand Out from the Crowd

So far, you've learned that investing in real estate can lead to financial freedom. And you've learned that you can say yes to financial fulfillment and spiritual fulfillment at the same time. Now, I'd like to teach you a little bit about how the opportunities you'll see from InvestingWithPurpose.org are different than a lot of other investment opportunities on the market.

At Integrity Holdings Group, we get asked a lot, "What makes you different? Who are you?"

Before I dive into those questions, I think it's important to first delineate the difference between public markets and private markets and how investing in each is different.

When you talk to your financial advisors about real estate investment, you could be talking about a Real Estate Investment Trust (REIT). And that's a product that they can sell you on an open, public market.

A couple of the caveats to be aware of with this type of product is that you're not a K-1 owner, which means you're getting a 1099 on the income that you're earning from that trust. Make sure that you're looking at the tax ramifications of investing in public markets and these types of products.

A K-1 represents a partnership return and signifies your ownership in the real estate investment. As a partner, you directly own a stake in the property, entitling you to both income and tax advantages associated with commercial real estate investments.

When you invest in a private opportunity (like you do with us), you get that K-1 at tax time and you get a private placement memorandum, which discloses all of these advantages and risks to you.

I will go a little bit more in-depth about tax advantages and our private placement memorandum in the Frequently Asked Questions Chapter of this book. But I hope this gives you a basic understanding of public versus private real estate investments.

What Makes Integrity Holdings Group Different

There are a lot of companies doing similar things to what we're doing, creating investment opportunities through real estate syndications. You can go invest with other operators just as easily as you can invest with us.

However, there are a couple of things I want you to be aware of that make us different from all the other operators in real estate investment.

The way that our investors get paid is the debt (the mortgage) gets paid on every property first, the preferred return goes to the investors second, and then we get paid last as the operator. And the reason we do that is because we have to hit a certain rate of return before we, as operators, are allowed to make any money. We even have a clawback provision in our private placement memorandum that if we're not hitting that target number of return, then we (the operators) owe the fund (or the deal) from our profit and proceeds to get the investors the number we promised them.

We have a very clear investment philosophy, a decision-making tool that we call the Big Three:

- One, we want to make sure we're not losing money, right? That's **preservation of capital**.

- Two, we want to make sure we can get our money back. That's **return of capital**.

- And three, we want to make a good return, or a good profit, which is **return on investment**.

When we're putting deals together, we look at properties with those three things in mind, in that order, to know if we're able to pay our investors, assuming that cash flow is available. Sometimes, there are reasons that cash flow is not available to pay the preferred return. The lack of cash flow doesn't mean that you're not going to get the return. It just means the return might be deferred until a later time.

Since we don't make money until we've hit the targeted rate of return, offering these preferred rates of return keeps us honest and working hard on behalf of our investors.

Also, at Invest with Purpose, we do monthly distributions instead of quarterly distributions. It's a lot more accounting for us to give monthly distribution, but we all like the regular passive cash flow. Most operators only offer quarterly payments.

But ultimately, I would say the main thing that separates us from all other operators is the heart behind the business, the investing-with-purpose idea.

The investing-with-purpose idea came from us trying to figure out how to give more abundantly to causes that we believe in before we "make it." At first, giving even 1% of our profits was a struggle. A lot of prayer went into making the decision to give even that 1%.

But the truth is that we're a tithing company. We tithe, meaning we give 10% of our profits away first, and then we give the tithe. At first, we gave 1% and past the tithe to a nonprofit. And that's where the idea all started. The next deal, we gave 2%. The next deal, we gave 4%. Our giving has been increasing ever since. The last deal we did, we gave more away than I could have ever imagined! And we're still aiming to increase our giving!

The goal for us is to fund nonprofits around the world and to fund different ministries so that we can make an impact on the world. We believe that impact investing is really the beginning of success. We believe that we have a duty to take care of those less fortunate than we are, and this vehicle gives us a great way to give back.

The cool thing about investing with purpose the way we do it is that giving back doesn't affect investor returns. We give out of corporate profits, and that's the real *why* for us. Real estate is the *what*. Giving back is the *why*.

And we're always really excited to share those updates on giving with our investors as we continue to do these deals. The same way we share the profits, we also share the good news about the work we're doing around the world. This giving is a big part of how we share the financial and spiritual wealth with all of our investors.

In a later chapter, we'll do a deeper dive into the InvestingWithPurpose.org philosophy about giving back through our non-profit partners. In the next chapter, however, I want to teach you more about the Big Three (preserving capital, return of capital, and return on investment) and educate you about how to choose good deals.

"The Lord loves a cheerful giver."

Chapter 4
Shoot for the Big Three

In this chapter, I want to dig deeper into the Big Three. We'll take a look at what goes into a real estate investment deal and how we choose profitable properties.

At InvestingWithPurpose.org, we use a powerful framework to look at every deal. We call this framework the Big Three, and it looks like this:

1. **Preservation of Capital:** Warren Buffett famously said, "Rule number one, never lose money. Rule number two, never forget rule number one." So, the first question we ask ourselves is, "How do we not lose money in this deal?"

2. **Return of Capital:** How do we get our money back out of a deal? Is it through a sale? Is it through a refinance? How do we get our money back?

3. **Return on Investment:** What is the rate of return that we can expect to make on this deal or investment?

Think of each item and question in the Big Three as a lens. First, we do our best to make sure we don't lose money. Then, we make sure we can get our money back in various scenarios. Finally, we make sure our investment returns are worthwhile to us and our investors.

This is important because most operators will start by telling you about item three, Return on Investment. Well, the truth is that anybody can talk about return of investment. But if operators can't accomplish item one and item two first, then you shouldn't listen to what they have to say about return on investment.

Since our goal is to effectively serve our investors, we use this process to make sure we're solid on items one and two before even considering item three! At the time of this writing, we've used this process to vet and underwrite thousands of deals and over $1 billion dollars in assets.

With all this in mind, you may be thinking...

How Do We Make Sure We're Solid on All Three Items Before Making a Deal?

For item one, Preservation of Capital, we thoroughly vet each and every acquisition through our stringent proprietary stress-testing process, which complements the standard checks and balances utilized within our industry. Our goal is to have a balance of low-volatility, solid-return deals while underwriting through a conservative position.

For item two, Return of Capital, we ensure multiple exit strategies exist on properties held by the fund in order to return capital to the investor.

Just in case you're not familiar with the term "exit," it is exactly what it sounds like. We make sure we have multiple strategies to sell or exit the property that will get the return of capital that we want for our investors.

For item three, Return on Investment, our rigorous asset and property management protocols are designed to maximize potential property value appreciation to investors and enhance overall investment returns.

And if you remember from Chapter 3, we even have a clawback clause in our private placement memorandum that states that we as operators don't get to make any money until we are paying our investors the preferred rates in our private placement memorandum.

As you can see, we use the Big Three to thoroughly vet the properties that we make deals on. The big reason we can so confidently help investors grow that all-important passive income is because…

We Invest in Stable, Low-Risk Properties That (In Theory) Only Appreciate Over Time

In the Integrity Holdings Group Opportunity Fund (IHG Opportunity Fund) – the fund that Invest with Purpose manages – we focus heavily on giving our investors peace of mind. The Fund is structured to provide consistent monthly returns, strong growth, limited volatility, and tax benefits to our investors. Our focus is in primary and secondary markets within the Sun Belt and Midwest regions of the United States. Specifically, we acquire and sell the following four types of properties within the fund.

- **Multi-Family Apartment Complexes:** Multifamily apartments are a good investment because they offer a reliable source of income through rental payments. Additionally, the demand for rental housing tends to remain steady regardless of economic conditions, which provides stability during market fluctuations. Moreover, investing in multifamily apartments allows for economies of scale, meaning expenses such as maintenance and property management can be spread across multiple units, thereby increasing profitability.

- **Self-Storage Facilities:** Self-storage facilities are a good investment because they offer low operating costs and high profit margins. These facilities require minimal maintenance and labor costs and can generate significant rental income with relatively low overhead expenses. Additionally, the demand for storage space tends to remain steady, even during economic downturns, making it a reliable investment option.

- **Senior Housing (i.e., assisted living facilities and nursing homes, etc.):** Senior housing is a good investment because it caters to a growing demographic that requires specialized housing options. As the baby boomer generation ages, the demand for senior housing is expected to increase, providing a stable source of rental income. Additionally, many senior housing facilities offer a range of services and amenities that can all generate higher rental rates and attract long-term tenants.

- **Student Housing (on major college or university campuses that house 25,000 students or more):** Student housing is a good investment because it caters to a stable and consistent demographic, with many students requiring off-campus housing options. Additionally, student housing often allows for higher rental rates due to the demand for amenities and services. With long-term leases and predictable rental income, student housing can offer a reliable source of cash flow for investors.

Investing in these types of properties and using the Big Three to evaluate each deal is how we ensure that we're getting the best cash flow opportunities for our investors.

Of course, this is just the high-level view of this process. Let's drill down and look at a real-life case study.

Case Study: Nampa, Idaho

We recently put together an investment deal for a multi-family apartment complex in Nampa, Idaho. The property has 172 units housed in 41, two-story residential buildings with 357 parking spaces. Of those parking spaces, 185 are single, open spaces, 175 are covered, and 22 are handicapped parking spaces. There's a fitness center, a clubhouse, a beautiful pool area, and a dog park. Some features in the units include granite countertops in the kitchen area, modern cabinets, and in-unit washers and dryers.

The first point I want to make here is that we invested in a quality property in a good area. We didn't invest in some run-down property that would need tons of capital to rehab and rent. And we didn't invest in a place where no one would want to live.

In addition, since real estate is hyper-local, we want to make sure that we're buying in areas that are growing. Frankly, I don't know if we could get a more economically viable growth spot than just outside of Boise, Idaho. I was amazed by the level of class-A construction that was going on everywhere. Not only that, but millions of square feet of manufacturing and industrial buildings (like Amazon warehouses) were being built right near the property. And there are also so many great restaurants and shops in the area near the complex.

Knowing all this, let's use the Big Three to decide on this property.

Preservation of Capital

The first question we asked was, "How do we not lose money in this deal?"

For this property, we're looking at a multi-family apartment complex, so we need to make sure we can either increase rents over time or make sure that even if rents stay stagnant, we can still make money.

Based on the fact that this was a long-term, fixed debt and not a volatile debt (i.e., the debt isn't going to change or fluctuate unexpectedly over time), and because area is blowing up around the apartment complex, the answer for this property in Nampa was a resounding 'yes, we will not lose money.' We assumed a loan with an interest rate of 2.88% for the next 7.5 years. Incredible loan terms, especially in today's climate.

In addition, we also felt that this was an extremely safe deal because the apartment was already at 97% occupancy. Meaning, we had people in the apartments paying rent! In fact, when we initially did our site visit, there were only two units available to tour, and those units were already pre-leased.

And to make it even safer, we discovered that there's not a lot of turnover at this apartment complex. People are staying because it's beautiful and the complex is adding amenities.

So, the tenants are already loving it!

All of these safety factors contribute to that preservation of capital.

Return of Capital

The second question we asked was, "How do we get our money back out of a deal?"

First, based on how much the mortgage was going to cost and how much the rent roll currently was, we could calculate the debt service coverage ratio (DSCR) and know what our return on capital was going to be.

Second, since there are very few other complexes that can compete with us in the area and very little competition that can accommodate the number of renters and provide the number of amenities that we can, we were very confident that renters would continue to occupy the complex and continue to pay rent (even if it was raised).

All of these factors were important to consider because they were indicators that we could easily sell the property and have a profitable exit strategy.

Return on Investment

The last question we ask is, "What is the rate of return that we can expect to make on this deal?"

Luckily this is just a simple calculation. We're always conservative in how we underwrite deals. So, when we looked at this property, and we saw that we could easily hit our rent projections, we felt confident in what we could expect our return-on-investment projection to be.

I hope getting to see how we apply the Big Three to a real-life deal gives you a better idea of how we operate. The bottom line is that we always put our investors and our communities first! And we're always excited to hunt out and add new deals to the Fund for you.

"We always put our investors and our communities first!"

Chapter 5
Establish Your Mission Money Matrix

The world has lied to you. It has told you that you are not smart enough to manage your own money. Further, the world has convinced you that you should delegate your stewardship to someone else, a person who likely does not make decisions on your behalf based on your worldview.

That's why, in this chapter, I'm going to give you some specific steps to follow so you can see firsthand if your investments align with your values or not. And then I'm going to give you the tools to make those choices for yourself instead of relying on a financial advisor.

To start this process, let's look at how your current investments line up with your core values. Whether you know it or not, all of your investments are supporting an agenda. So, whose agenda are you supporting? Where are those investment dollars going? What are they being used for? And what kind of impact are those dollars creating?

Admittedly, this will take some time because you'll need to do a little bit of research on how your investment dollars are being used. Don't worry, though. I'll give you the tools to do this in a moment.

First, I want you to realize how important this concept is. In my experience, I've discovered that most investors do not know what their money is being used for. For example, when you invest in the stock market, did you know that you actually own a piece of the companies you're invested in? You do!

But think about that. If you own a piece of each company, then you're also responsible for the actions that company is taking. So, it just makes sense that you should know and understand the mission, vision, beliefs, and culture that drive that company. After all, your money is (at least in some way) responsible for the outcomes of that investment.

At InvestingWithPurpose.org, we believe Christians have been investing in companies that create a decent rate of return, but they haven't looked at their eternal legacy. They are unknowingly funding depravity and perversion rather than the things that honor God.

As Christian leaders, we're always looking at whether or not the investments in our portfolios and the properties in the IHG Opportunity Fund align with our worldview.

Regardless of your worldview, I think it's important that this kind of responsible stewardship also be at the forefront of your mind. In other words, I think it's important that you have an investment strategy that aligns with your core values. Otherwise, you are just putting money into the stock market (or some other investment) and hoping for a good retirement without realizing the impact your money is having on the world around you.

Listen, most people have been taught to look at return on investment over impact in the world. But we believe that your investments can do both. You can get a healthy return on your investment while making an impact on the people around you!

So how do we do it? How do we make sure that we're getting good returns while being responsible stewards at the same time? Introducing…

The Mission Money Matrix

The Mission Money Matrix is very simple. But don't let its simplicity fool you. Used correctly, this is a powerful tool that can help you manage your investments responsibly.

Take a look at the figure shown on page 52.

The horizontal line (X axis) represents your profit potential (i.e., your potential return on investment). The vertical line (Y axis) represents your mission alignment (i.e., how well your investments align with your worldview).

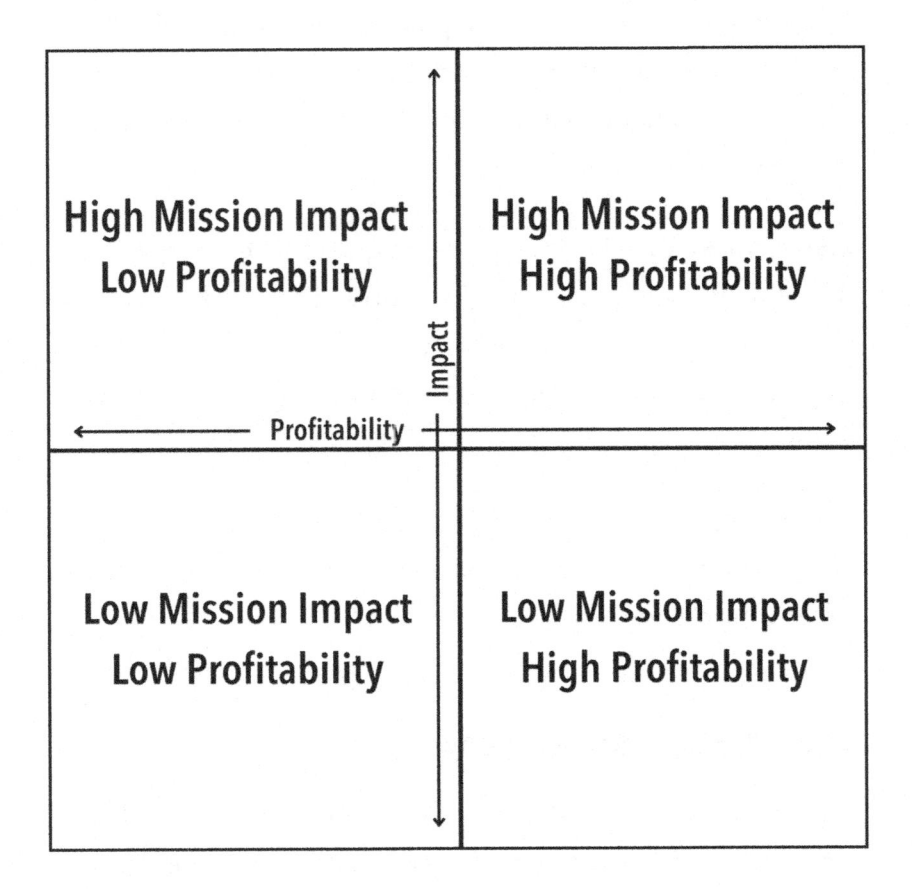

High Mission Impact **Low Profitability**	**High Mission Impact** **High Profitability**
Low Mission Impact **Low Profitability**	**Low Mission Impact** **High Profitability**

Vertical axis: Impact
Horizontal axis: Profitability

The Mission Money Matrix
A powerful tool to help you manage your investments responsibly

The farther to the right an investment is on the X axis, the greater the potential return on investment is. Likewise, the farther up on the Y axis an investment is, the more aligned with your values that investment is.

In a moment, I'd like to offer you some suggestions on how to use this matrix. But first, I want to point out two things.

First, if you've never thought about your investment alignment like this, it's okay. It's not your fault. No one has ever taught you this way of thinking. But now that you understand the importance of aligning your investments with your values, you'll never see another investment the same way again.

Second, aligning your investments with your worldview is not going to be a light switch. Everything is not going to align immediately. But having thoughts like this on your radar and thinking like this long-term is going to help you make more profitable and more satisfying decisions about your financial future.

With that said, let's look at the quadrants of The Mission Money Matrix and see what each one means.

Top Right Quadrant

The top right quadrant contains investments that have a high mission alignment and high profit potential at the same time. Ideally, this is where you want to have most or all of your investments. If you have current investments that fit into this quadrant, you'll want to invest more attention and resources into these investments to continue to grow them.

If you share the same ideals as we do at InvestingWithPurpose.org, then you'll find that our investments with us fit into this quadrant.

Top Left Quadrant

The top left quadrant contains investments that have a high mission alignment but have less profit potential. While you'll want to keep these investments and celebrate them, you'll also want to try to contain the costs (i.e., invest less money in this asset) to maximize your profit potential.

Bottom Right Quadrant

The bottom right quadrant contains investments that have a lower mission alignment but higher profit potential. For these investments, you'll want to keep trying to grow that investment with more money. However, you may also want to see if you can figure out a way to increase the impact through those investments.

For example, could you increase the impact of that investment by contributing portions of your profit to a donor-advised fund, like we've implemented at Integrity Holdings Group?

Bottom Left Quadrant

The bottom left quadrant contains investments that have a low mission alignment and low profit potential. They don't align with your mission. They don't align with your vision. And they don't align with making profit. So, take the steps to get rid of these investments, so you can invest in other vehicles that rank in the top right quadrant of The Mission Money Matrix.

Tools to Plot Your Misson Money Matrix

I know we've covered a lot in this chapter. So, to make this as easy as possible for you, here are some tools to help you plot your investments into the Money Matrix.

NOTE: *It's important for you to know these are just examples. I, in fact, have zero dollars in the stock market. I'm showing you these tools so you can start to make your own decisions about the dollars you are investing.*

For investments in the stock market, we've found a great company called Fintel (Ffintel.io). This is an investment research platform that gives you all kinds of useful information about companies listed on the stock exchange as well as lists of companies that are in specific funds and holdings.

To illustrate this point, I recently went to Fintel and pulled up Berkshire Hathaway. They're one of the biggest investors in the stock market. At the time of this writing, Fintel showed that Berkshire Hathaway had a portfolio value somewhere around $895 billion.

I was given information about the top 100 holdings (or companies) inside Berkshire Hathaway's portfolio. 51% of its entire portfolio is Apple. Berkshire Hathaway holds 915 million shares of Apple, which has a value of somewhere in the vicinity of $176 billion.

Now, if I'm invested in Berkshire Hathaway's mutual fund, and it owns shares in Apple, I would also (in this hypothetical example) own a piece of Apple. If I'm truly living up to responsible stewardship, I am responsible for how that company acts since some of my money is going to help them fund their business.

So that's how Fintel can help you. This website can help you drill down to see what you actually own shares in so that you may determine whether those investments align with your values.

Another great tool that I've found is OpenSecrets (OpenSecrets.org). This is a great website to help you figure out which companies are funding political causes or donating to campaign funds. This website's main mission is to track money in American politics and create transparency around that money. It's a great website to see where corporations and the individuals who work in those corporations are donating to so you can make sure that those donations align with your worldview.

Because remember, if you're invested in a company, your investment is going to fund that company and pay those salaries. If those employees and corporations are donating to causes against your values, you are indirectly funding those causes as well.

Let's revisit Apple.

On OpenSecrets, I learned that Apple is ranked 43 out of 9,073 companies in 2022 in terms of lobbying. And they gave about $9.3 million away to politicians and political causes. I'm not going to list all of the individuals and organizations here. My point is that you can see quite clearly who those contribution dollars are flowing to.

Beyond using Fintel and OpenSecrets, I would also encourage you to visit the websites of the individual companies in which you are invested to see if they support or damage your core values.

Again, if I visit Apple's website, I can get an idea of what that company is doing with its money.

In 2022, Apple gave away $880 million, and its employees logged 2 million volunteer hours. That $880 million was spread over 44,000 organizations globally.

My main point here is that the information you need to make smart decisions is out there. You just need to seek out that information and ask yourself, "Does this company align with my values?" Then, once you seek out the information, plot the investment on The Mission Money Matrix and determine how you'll proceed with that specific investment.

As you can see, this is a really important concept to start thinking through. What am I stewarding? How am I stewarding my cash?

I hope that knowing you can invest in companies that share your values is an "aha!" moment for you. I know it was for me. You can earn good returns while also making the impact you want to make!

Okay, it's time to see how you're stewarding your money. For every investment you're making (or going to make), plot it into The Mission Money Matrix. Is that investment mission-aligned? Is that investment profit-aligned? Or is that investment both?

I don't know if you can tell, but this topic pumps me up! I'm so excited for you, and I'm very grateful to be with you on this journey to financial freedom through Biblical stewardship.

Now that you have the tools and knowledge to refine your investment criteria, you can be a great steward while making great profits!

"It's important that you have an investment strategy that aligns with your core values."

Chapter 6
Invest with Purpose

One of the core values behind InvestingWithPurpose.org is that we are Christ-minded. And to that end, we are a tithing company, meaning 10% of our profit (as operators) goes to a cause. We don't just invest for profit, we invest with purpose. Always.

We believe that we're meant to fund righteousness with our success and support people and causes that share our core values. We want to be the tribe you come to for support in growing your core values. Because what happens when you are trying to be a good steward and you are trying to fund righteousness, but you are in a tribe of people who don't share your values? You meet a lot of resistance, right? You are forced to defend your choices and maybe even defend your values.

That's a major hurdle to get over if you're trying to align your investments with your core values and make a real impact in the world.

The truth is that God is calling us to do so much more. And as Christians, we need to start rowing together to get the job done.

You see, the problem right now is that some of the people who are in the position to finance things and invest money are financing perversion and wickedness. And it's our responsibility as Christians to reach into our nation and our culture to offset this imbalance because the righteous haven't prospered enough yet.

That's why I love real estate investing so much. Because it is a tool to help the righteous prosper. And for us at Integrity Holdings Group, we're focused on having a purpose-driven plan, being intentional with that plan, and executing that plan for the greatest profit and impact.

I feel like especially in the world of investment, people often talk about how they're focused on a good return. Focusing on a good return is great. But I think we need to be focused on creating generational and legacy wealth while also being focused on creating an eternal legacy. And I have personally found that these things are not mutually exclusive. In fact, there's a lot of symbiosis that comes through being purposeful and intentional about building wealth and building an eternal legacy.

What do I mean by that? I mean that everything you do should be aligned with your values. I've already talked a lot about creating core values and aligning with those values.

When you identify core values in your life, your family, your business, and your investments, you are being purposeful and intentional about lining those values up with your life and your money.

And that's what we're all about. We're about being intentional about making an impact. We think a lot about the intersection of marketplace and ministry, faith and finance, and how we can create a good return while creating a big impact. We want to be intentional with where our dollars flow so that we know what agendas we are supporting.

The genesis of our investing-with-purpose philosophy began when a missionary coming back from the Philippines asked to meet with my wife and me. The missionary was coming over to raise support for her mission trips, and her visit happened to be the week of Christmas. I remember sitting around the kitchen table as she explained about the people she was helping and the pain those people were in. During this presentation, I realized that the missionary was using her time that was meant for rest and relaxation back home in the States (during Christmastime, no less) to raise money that would fund her work in the field. This situation really bothered me. As a business owner, I thought, *Why are the people on the front lines having to raise this money? Where are the businesspeople? Why aren't the businesspeople helping raise the money?*

When you invest with us, it's pretty clear what you're supporting. We put our money in position so that we can make sure that we're getting under the spout where the glory comes out and support the people on the front lines for God.

And we support that mission for glory with a three-pronged approach. First, we put our money where our mouths are, and we tithe. Second, we make a conscious effort to support community building in our communities. And third, we support God's mission by doing evangelical work in our communities.

As you already know, we're a tithing company. At the beginning of this real estate investing journey, I was in prayer, and I wanted to know how to give more abundantly *now*, before we "made it," before we had become truly financially successful. God made it simple. Partner with Him on every deal. Start by giving 1% of the profit to a non-profit.

We give through our donor-advised fund, and we all tithe from our paychecks as well. Now, that first year we got started, the offering past the tithe wasn't very much. It was about $1800 total. The next deal we did, we raised the offering to 2%. The deals after that, we were able to keep raising the giving: 4%, 8%. And we aim to increase that number as we grow. The entire amount of giving is made from company profits that go into a donor-advised fund, which funds ministries around the world. Our goal is to eventually give more than 50%! So, we're in the fight for sure.

We're using our dollars to get into the cultural battles that we're dealing with here at home in America. And we're doing amazing work abroad with people in other countries as well. Last year alone, we paid our investors over $1 million in profit while we were also giving away money through the donor-advised fund. As of this writing, we've supported over 35 different ministries around the world that have impacted over 250,000 lives.

Not only do we use our mission to impact lives around the world with our donor-advised fund and the money we raise, the support we offer to the people in our communities is really boots-on-the-ground-for-glory type stuff.

The next prong in our strategy to support the people on the front lines for God is our partnership with a faith-based nonprofit called Apartment Life. Through our partnership with them, we set aside one or two apartments per asset we acquire. Apartment Life gets a free apartment that they fill with an onsite community coordinator. These community coordinators arrange events for residents with two goals in mind. These events help residents connect to one another and make friends, so they feel happier and more fulfilled. And these events also connect residents to local churches so the churches can minister the needs of the community.

There are two goals of every Apartment Life program: to provide real business value to apartment owners and to have a positive impact on people's lives. Research shows that

Apartment Life adds a huge financial benefit to the average community through reduced resident and staff turnover as well as increased leasing. And the value added for residents through an increased sense of community can't be understated.

Prong three in this strategy is to engage a local church to "adopt" our community. We work with the local church to implement a multi-family ministry. Right now, 37% of all Americans live in multi-family housing. And 90% to 95% of these families are unchurched. This is an amazing opportunity to grow God's Kingdom through onsite and local ministries.

These ministries are the bridge between the community and the church. They have so much opportunity to serve in this way. Some examples of this ministry include prayer walking the community, bible studies in conference rooms we provide, tutoring for children during the summer to make sure they keep up in school, oil changes for single moms in the complex, cooking classes, women's groups, youth groups, barbecues, and so much more! Really just being the light.

I don't just want asset management reports that show pro forma versus actuals on rental growth and rental rates. I want to know how many people are getting invited to church, how many people are asking for prayer, and how many salvations we have in the complex.

When you look around our country, right now, I think most of you would agree that our country is drifting dangerously away from the Christian principles that it was founded upon. In many spheres of culture, the enemy is having a field day. We have to create wealth ourselves and redirect our wealth to Godly influences.

So, seeing those numbers is truly a dream come true.

Billy Graham prophesied the next major move of God was going to be in the marketplace. And we believe that major move is going into real estate. That's why we do what we do. And that's why we position Christians to make real change and real impact in the marketplace and the world.

"The truth is that God is calling us to do so much more."

Chapter 7
Invest for Impact

At InvestingWithPurpose.org, real estate investing is our *what*, and building the Kingdom is our *why*.

We are firm believers in the principle of "doing well by doing good." First, we do this by setting aside double-digit gifting out of *our* profits, not out of *your* profits. So, by simply investing with us, you are helping expand our impact, and you're increasing your impact as well.

But wait, there's more! We also offer our investors an opportunity to contribute to the meaningful work our partners are doing in the world. That way, together, we can expand our reach and expand the Kingdom.

As I mentioned in the last chapter, to date we've supported over 35 different nonprofits around the world to date, which has translated into hundreds of thousands of lives being impacted. The rest of this chapter is devoted to some of our current nonprofit partners, so you can see how we help them make a difference in our communities here in American as well as raise awareness and grow the Kingdom around the world.

Heroes International

Heroes International is a collaborative charity bringing life-changing relief to orphans, widows, and the disadvantaged.

They believe in the dignity of offering hands-up, not handouts, for those with able bodies and minds. Jobs for those able to work, and charity for all others. Capitalism with a conscience, and a revival of morals, are indeed the only forces that have ever vanquished poverty and brought about systemic redemption.

In addition to their solo projects, their shared pursuit of making the world a better place leads us to take great pride in finding front-line heroes in the world's most desperate places, partnering with them, and helping empower them through various means (financial and otherwise) in their life-saving work.

You can learn more about their work by visiting HeroesInternational.org.

World Missions Outreach

Their heart's desire is to reach the people of Nicaragua by meeting their spiritual, educational, and physical needs.

World Missions Outreach has partnered with 70 churches across Nicaragua. Each church provides an opportunity for children to receive a hot, nutritious meal every day. World Mission's Outreach (WMO) serves 15,000 meals every day. That's more than 5.4 million meals per year!

You can learn more about their work by visiting WMOC.org.

Love Life

Love Life is the call to mobilize a Christian witness to every abortion center across America. God is highlighting the 700 abortion clinics in our nation as being legitimate mission fields that are worthy of our attention, time, and resources. However, out of the 700 abortion centers in America, only 200 of these clinics have a consistent, Christian witness.

Love Life America believes these abortion mission fields deserve the attention of full-time missionaries as well as a network of local churches. Our strategy is to equip and resource Love Life Sidewalk Missionaries to bring the hope of Jesus and the help of His Church to these places of death. Alongside sending missionaries, they also train and equip local churches to be Houses of Refuge for people to run to for long-term care and discipleship.

You can learn more about their work by visiting LoveLife.org.

The Gateway Project at Eagles' Wings Ministries

The Gateway Project at Eagles' Wings Ministries is a partnership of individuals, teams, churches, and organizations that work together to see the least reached people on the earth reached with the Gospel. Through Gateway Academy, a five-month missions training program based in Southeast Asia, the Gateway Project is training teams of leaders to go to the least reached, most strategic cities across Asia and the Middle East. The Passarellas serve as Hub directors based in Thailand, training leaders for world missions. This initiative will train hundreds of American and Asian Leaders to reach people from the Great Wall in the Far East along the Silk Road to the Western Wall in Jerusalem.

You can learn more about their work by visiting EaglesWings.org/team/mark-passarella.

F.I.R.E International – Beauty for Ashes

Beauty for Ashes is a ministry dedicated to training, equipping, and restoring those currently working in the sex industry or survivors rescued from sex trafficking. This restoration occurs through education in a wide variety of entrepreneurial skills as well as the creation of a safe place to recover and be restored mentally, spiritually, and emotionally. Their team is comprised of local Filipinos, international staff, and volunteers from various churches and organizations.

You can learn more about their work by visiting Fire-International.org/zimmerman-jeryl.

Antioch Ministries International

Antioch Ministries International exists to be a catalyst for a sweeping move of the Spirit of God that ignites revival in the church and to see church planting movements in every sphere of society. It is their desire that the nation of Thailand and peoples of Southeast Asia (11 countries) be brought to Christ through church planting movements and that God would be revealed to those peoples through the power of the Holy Spirit in signs and wonders.

The ministries are committed to prayer for revival in their own lives and in the lives of Thai believers, evangelism, discipling new believers, as well as training and sending out national leaders. These ministries are spokes of the hub they are planting in Chiang Mai, Thailand.

You can learn more about their work by visiting Antioch.org.

Kingdom Alive

There is a consensus among the First Nations Prayer Group that God has a special calling upon the First Nations people at this juncture in time. It is their belief that the First Nations are a sleeping giant who are awakening and are key to church revival. God has reserved them as powerful evangelists around the world. The Chinese Christians have a unique burden for First Nations as a type of midwives to birth this movement of God among First Nations. The Chinese Christians are family with us and partners in aiding First Nations

Christians to accomplish God's purposes. First Nation Christians have joined together in love, trust, and perseverance.

Toms River Field of Dreams

Toms River Field of Dreams' mission is to provide communities in Monmouth and Ocean Counties an all-inclusive complex with a playground and other physical and cognitive environments that recognize everyone's right to fully participate in equitable play. This inclusive complex intentionally addresses the physical and social inclusion of people of all ages and abilities.

Toms River and its surrounding communities also benefit from being the only area in New Jersey with a complex specifically developed for special needs individuals. It serves as a sustainable landmark and a significant accomplishment for the town. As an open, public space, the TRFOD is an inclusive environment for the entire community to enjoy all year round.

You can learn more about their work by visiting TomsRiverFieldOfDreams.com.

The Blessings Project

The Blessings Project empowers small communities and forgotten people in remote regions of the world to help them thrive and grow once again. They build schools and small medical clinics, provide education, and introduce renewable resources geared towards development.

You can learn more about their work by visiting TheBlessingProjects.org.

Promise Keepers

Promise Keepers is committed to connecting men across all denominational, generational, racial, and cultural lines. Conferences, local gatherings, and virtual events give men across the world access to an unprecedented hub of Christian resources. Additionally, the PK App provides anytime access to Bible studies, sermons, and practical courses developed by PK's incredible partner organizations and ministries, as well as the best Promise Keepers content from the last 30 years. Topics include fatherhood, marriage, faith, and mental health, with additional topics and resources added regularly.

What's more, virtual events and everything in the PK App are free to individuals and churches. Men's groups host local gatherings throughout the year, using resources geared specifically towards men and the issues they care about. Promise Keepers also helps connect churches with larger organizations like Prison Fellowship for even greater outreach and ministry opportunities.

You can learn more about their work by visiting PromiseKeepers.org.

Tim Tebow Foundation

The Christian faith is about loving Jesus and loving people, and that is what The Tim Tebow Foundation works to do through outreach. Whether it is spending a weekend encouraging a child with a life-threatening illness, helping a family adopt an international child with special needs, crowning kings and queens at the prom, or showing God's love through their four other outreaches, their goal is to let people know that God loves all people and all people are worthy.

You can learn more about their work by visiting TimTebowFoundation.org.

Together for Israel

Together for Israel is a non-profit ministry that exists to fulfill the biblical mandate to support those laboring in the land of Israel. We support the believers in Israel by unashamedly raising funds that specifically go to those who are laboring in the Land for the Gospel.

You can learn more about their work by visiting TogetherForIsrael.org.

Bayside Chapel

Bayside Chapel's mission is to bring glory to God by leading people into fruitful relationships with Jesus Christ.

The church's vision is to be so transformed by Christ that He will send its congregants out to transform communities in His name.

They value the Word of God because it is vital to a transformed life. They value prayer as an expression of their utter dependence upon God. They value relationships that lead us to maturity in Christ. They value putting people on mission to reach others for Christ.

Bayside Chapel missions include church-planting initiatives, community groups, counseling, and missionary work.

You can learn more about the work by visiting BaysideChapel.org.

Grace Church

Grace Church's mission is giving God glory and bringing people into relationship with Christ. Their vision is for all people in Hickory, North Carolina and the surrounding area to experience the grace of God through Jesus Christ.

Dedicated to generosity, Grace Church encourages active giving within the church and beyond. Other core values are loyalty in outreach to the community, authenticity in worship, The Word of God, prayer, unity in connecting the body of Christ, and stewardship of time, talents, and treasures.

You can learn more about their work by visiting GraceChurch.tv.

Christian Renewal Church

Christian Renewal Church is a Spirit-filled Church that is committed to a lifestyle of sacrificial love, bringing genuine heart transformation to the generations in our midst. They are passionate about reaching the Lowcountry with the gospel of Jesus, and they celebrate His love for us. They are an authentic, hungry church that seeks out the hurting, broken, and lost to meet Jesus. CRC is after a lifestyle of prayer and surrender that serves one purpose: to bring God's glory.

You can learn more about their work by visiting ChristianRenewalChurch.org.

Catalyst Church

Catalyst Church's mission is to lead every person to know God, find freedom, discover purpose, and make a difference.

They're vision is to build the lives of people by following the ways of Jesus, leading to the renewal of our world.

They believe that Jesus is the foundation of your life and everything you do. They believe we are better together, and we are not meant to go through life alone. They believe growth is your responsibility, and you change the world by allowing God to change your world. Spiritual growth is a byproduct of your relationship with God. They believe service should be your posture, and they exist to serve their community the same way Jesus did. They feel called to follow His example. And they believe that Monday is their mission. They are called to follow Jesus and fulfill His mission every day of the week in every sphere of life.

You can learn more about their work by visiting YourCatalystChurch.com.

The Ashley Lauren Foundation

The Ashley Lauren Foundation's goal is to ease families' pediatric cancer journeys by providing direct financial, material, and emotional assistance, along with many programs to bring smiles to the children.

You can learn more about their work by visiting AshleyLaurenFoundation.org.

The Kylie Rowand Foundation

The Kylie Rowand Foundation is dedicated to raising awareness of and providing support for children and their families directly affected by childhood cancer. They strive to make the lives of the patients and family members a little less stressful by supporting their needs and addressing their struggles.

The Foundation was inspired by a two-year-old girl named Kylie who courageously fought stage-four neuroblastoma for 13 months. In February of 2015, Kylie flew home to be with the Lord. During her battle, Kylie infectiously gained support, prayer, and love from hundreds of thousands of people across the globe. It is now up to us to come together to help finish Kylie's fight.

You can learn more about their work by visiting KylieStrong.org.

Aeriel Recovery

Aeriel Recovery's mission is to save lives and stop evil. To date, Aerial Recovery has rescued over 7,500 people across 20 countries.

Aerial Recovery trains and deploys Humanitarian Special Operators to effectively respond to natural and man-made disasters and combat sex trafficking. Deploying teams made up of Veterans and First Responders from their Heal the Heroes Initiative, Aerial tackles some of the most difficult rescue and response missions across the globe.

You can learn more about their work by visiting AerialRecovery.org.

Grassroots Crisis Intervention

Grassroots Crisis Intervention provides 24/7 access to individuals and families for behavioral health, crisis, and homeless services.

You can learn more about their work by visiting GrassrootsCrisis.org.

Hope Inspire Love

Hope Inspire Love is an anti-human-trafficking nonprofit that exists to eradicate human trafficking and sexual exploitation in our communities. They provide awareness opportunities, prevention initiatives, education curriculum for high school students and youth groups, advocacy, and job-skills training. Their flagship Hope Mentorship Program for at-risk teens, young adults, and survivors of sex trafficking is all about education and prevention. Together, they are empowering survivors of sex trafficking to flourish and thrive!

You can learn more about their work by visiting HopeInspireLove.org.

THINQ Media

In a world gripped by uncertainty and isolation, people are looking for trusted content and meaningful conversations. For two decades, THINQ Media has helped thousands of people think about the most pressing issues in culture and create conversations that lead to wisdom. With a vision to raise up one million thought leaders who will impact 100 million people in the next 10 years, THINQ works diligently to convene and educate the influencers, equip the Church, and mobilize the next generation to shape our culture and create a future rooted in biblical wisdom and hope.

You can learn more about their work by visiting ThinqMedia.com.

Child and Parental Right Campaign

As a non-partisan, non-profit, public-interest law firm, the Child & Parental Rights Campaign, Inc. was founded to respond to radical new gender identity ideology overtaking families and threatening the well-being of children and the fundamental right of parents.

You can learn more about their work by visiting ChildParentRights.org.

Making an Impact

While I can give you story after story about how our non-profit partners have helped us reach more people and create change in the world, I'd like to end this chapter with just one of my favorite stories.

A couple of years ago, when America was pulling out of Afghanistan, one of our nonprofit partners informed us about a group of Afghani refugees who were in danger of being killed because of the help they gave American soldiers.

They said, "The refugees have 757s on the ground, and they need jet fuel to get out of there." So, we did what we do. We helped! And because of this nonprofit partner, we were able to get them the jet fuel they needed, and they escaped to freedom!

I tear up when I tell this story. Because of the culture here at Integrity Holdings Group, and because of the amazing people and organizations we're able to partner with (investors, nonprofit partners, etc.), over 400 Afghani refugees were saved that day!

As you can clearly see, we take our impact on the world and on Christian causes very seriously. We pride ourselves on not just giving lip service to being good stewards but making a genuine impact for Christ.

We answer the call each and every day by cheerfully serving our investors with amazing real estate deals and then passionately giving to our amazing nonprofit partners (out of our own profits) to help those in need.

For an updated list of our nonprofit partners, go to InvestingWithPurpose.org/partners. There, you'll see who we're working with and what they're doing to help others around the globe.

In addition, you can hear more stories just like this on our Investing with Purpose podcast (InvestingWithPurpose.org/investing-with-purpose-podcast).

"We are firm believers in the principle of 'doing well by doing good.'"

Chapter 8
Frequently Asked Questions

Thank you so much for taking the time to read this book. I really hope that you got a lot out of it from both a financial and spiritual standpoint.

Before we end, I'd like to take this opportunity to cover some of the most frequently asked questions that we get at Integrity Holdings Group. If you truly are interested in investing in the IHG Opportunity Fund, a lot of this information will be useful to you.

Where Can I Find Your Legal/Income Disclaimer?

As I stated in the Author's Note at the beginning of this book, this book contains statements that are forward-looking within the meaning of the Private Securities Litigation Reform Act of 1995. These include statements regarding Integrity Holdings Group and the Integrity Holdings Group Opportunity

Fund, talking about our future growth, momentum, operations, market share, business outlook, and financial performance expectations. These statements are estimates only and actual results may ultimately differ from them. Except to the extent required by applicable security laws, we undertake no obligation to update or revise any of the forward-looking statements that you may read in this book.

You can find our full disclaimer at InvestingWithPurpose.org/disclaimer.

Who Can Invest with Us?

To invest in the IHG Opportunity Fund, you must be an accredited investor.

The Securities Exchange Commission (SEC) dictates who is accredited and who is not. The simplest definition is that you make $200,000 a year in income if you're filing as single and $300,000 a year if you're filing jointly. You also need to have $1 million in net worth outside of your primary residence, meaning you have stocks, bonds, mutual funds, savings accounts, checking accounts, or other real estate property that adds up to $1 million or above.

NOTE: If you hold some different professional licenses, you could be considered accredited as well. For example, if you have a Series 7, 65, or 82 broker-dealer licenses, you would be considered accredited. Or if you're a CPA, you could become an accredited investor through your professional accreditation.

Just so you know, even if you meet any of these requirements, the SEC doesn't send you a letter in the mail and say, "Hey, congratulations, you're accredited." You're simply accredited if you meet these requirements.

If you are still unclear about whether or not you meet the accreditation threshold, reach out to us at InvestingWithPurpose.org/book and we'll be happy to help.

Can You Invest with Us if You Are Not an Accredited Investor?

In the past, we've been able to extend certain investment opportunities to non-accredited investors on a case-by-case basis. The requirement to be a non-accredited investor with us is that you must have a substantive business relationship with Integrity Holdings Group.

What is a "substantive business relationship"? According to www.SEC.gov, "a 'substantive' relationship is formed when the entity offering securities (i.e., the company or its broker-dealer or investment adviser) has sufficient information to evaluate and evaluates a potential investor's status as an accredited investor."

In other words, if we don't know each other and you're just diving into this book to learn more about real estate investing, you'll have to sign up on our website for a call so that we can get to know each other, talk about your finances, and evaluate your status and eligibility as a potential investor.

To sign up for a call, you can visit InvestingWithPurpose.org/book.

Can You Invest with Us if You Live Outside the United States?

Yes. We work with international investors all the time. There are some tax holdbacks that we have to work out so that we know we're holding back the appropriate amount for taxes. But the short answer is yes.

If you have residency outside the United States and you're interested in finding out if investing with us is a good fit for you, reach out to us at InvestingWithPurpose.org/book.

Are There Tax Advantages to Investing with Us?

Yes, when you invest in the IHG Opportunity Fund, you get a K-1 (instead of a 1099) at tax time. A K-1 represents a partnership return, and it signifies your ownership in the real estate investment. As a partner, you directly own a stake in the property, entitling you to both income and tax advantages associated with commercial real estate investments.

If you have any more questions about a K-1 or the tax benefits of investing with us, reach out to us at InvestingWithPurpose.org/book.

What Is an REIT and How Is It Different from Investing with Us?

A real estate investment trust (REIT) is basically a Wall Street vehicle to raise capital and buy real estate. However, with a REIT, you are not the owner of that real estate. Instead, you are the owner of shares in a corporation that owns the real estate.

Most people who invest in an REIT think, *Oh, I invested in a "real estate investment trust," so I'm invested in real estate.* But that's not true. The corporation owns the underlying real estate asset.

In reality, an REIT is just a tax structure that defines who gets taxed on the profits from the real estate.

Are the Operators at Integrity Holdings Group Fiduciaries?

Yes, we are. Every decision that we make, we're a fiduciary for you as a fund manager. Being a fiduciary means that we have to make decisions in your best interest, not ours.

We want everyone to be aware that their existing financial advisor (depending on where they are in the country) may or may not be a fiduciary. Registered investment advisors (RIAs) are fiduciaries, but other financial advisors may not be. Make sure to find out!

As fiduciaries, we work on your behalf and must make decisions that are the best for you and your investments. Being a fiduciary is a big deal, and we take that responsibility seriously.

What Is a Private Placement Memorandum?

Simply put, a private placement memorandum is a contract between us and our investors. However, it is a very important document because it discloses all of your risks and tax liabilities, it grants exemption from registering the investment with the SEC, and it also ensures that Integrity Holdings Group is following the rules and regulations as if the investment were registered with the SEC.

This is a document that you would enter into with any private investment firm (like we are).

What Is a Clawback Provision?

This is a provision in our private placement memorandum that makes us special. Not many operators have a provision like this in their contracts.

Basically, this provision states that we, as operators, can't make any money until our investors are making the minimum preferred return. This provision is special because it means that all the profits go to you until that preferred return is met or exceeded. Only after that preferred return is met or exceeded can we collect any profit for ourselves.

If for some reason, an investment does not hit that preferred return and our company did make profit, the fund can "clawback" income until that preferred return is hit.

What Is a Preferred Return?

A preferred return in real estate investment is a predetermined rate of return that investors receive on their investment before profits are distributed to other stakeholders. It ensures investors receive a set level of profit and provides a safeguard against potential risks or uncertainties associated with the investment.

How Often Does Integrity Holdings Group Send out Distributions?

Monthly. We send out monthly distributions because we all love cash flow. The monthly distributions make our accounting department a little bit crazy here, but we all agree that monthly cash flow is the best way to build passive income.

What Are the Redemption Periods on Our Properties?

We underwrite properties to a five-year hold. If you don't think you can reasonably leave your money invested with us for that five-year period, then this investment opportunity might not be the best for you.

Honestly, if you pull your investment out at the two- or three-year mark, you're leaving a lot of money on the table. That's why we encourage our investors to stay in the investment for five to seven years. Those are the people who benefit from our investments the most.

What Is the Initial Investment with Us?

The short answer is that the minimum investment amount is $250,000.

But the long answer is that every investor is a little bit different, and depending on your situation, we may be flexible.

To learn more and have a conversation about what investment figure would work best for you, reach out to us at InvestingWithPurpose.org/book.

How Often Does Integrity Holdings Group Take on New Investors?

All investment opportunities are first come, first serve. We generally add new investors every 30 to 60 days. These investment opportunities tend to coincide with the closing of a property.

To learn more about our current opportunities and if you qualify to invest with us, reach out to us at InvestingWithPurpose.org/book.

"We don't just invest for profit, we invest with purpose. Always."

Your Next Steps

Congratulations! Just picking up this book and navigating your way to the end tells me that you are serious about growing generational wealth while making the biggest impact on the world that you can.

To recap, you've learned...

- How you can achieve financial independence through real estate,

- How you can align your investments with your core values, and

- How you can invest with purpose to make a major impact on the world around you!

It's my honor sharing this information with you. I pray this information has inspired you to take action toward investing with purpose. And I hope you truly take the time to let this information sink in and that you take the necessary action to vet us out, so you can make the best decision possible.

If you'd like to learn more about how you can invest with us and invest with purpose, go to InvestingWithPurpose.org/book.

- Steven Libman
Co-Founder and Managing Partner
at Integrity Holding Group
www.InvestingWithPurpose.org

About the Author

Steven Libman is the Co-Founder of InvestingWithPurpose.org and is one of the Managing Partners of Integrity Holdings Group. Prior to IHG, Steven began as a realtor, flipping almost 1,000 properties in the residential real estate space. After getting burned out in a very transactional, highly taxed business model, IHG moved into the multifamily and self-storage space to create passive, tax-advantaged income for themselves and their investors.

Steven has contributed to and been recognized by a number of industry publications including *Forbes*, and the *Top 100 in Real Estate*. IHG also runs a donor advised fund where it carves out a percentage of company income to create passive income for nonprofits around the world.

Steven has a B.A. from Boston University.

In his spare time, he focuses on spending time with his wife Grace and their three children, volunteering at his local church, and playing golf and tennis. A self-described foodie and personal-growth-focused entrepreneur, Steven has a desire to help people reach their own personal and investment goals through any means possible.

To learn more about Steven and the team at Integrity Holdings Group, go to InvestingWithPurpose.org/team.

About Integrity Holdings Group

Integrity Holdings Group invests in multiple real estate asset classes that are stable, low-risk properties that (in theory) only appreciate over time. We are committed to giving our members the ability to create generational wealth while avoiding the instability of the stock market. We also are committed to creating a positive impact on the world, through both our nonprofit partnerships and the properties that we manage.

In addition, Integrity Holdings Group is a Christian owned and operated company that believes in giving abundantly to help grow the Kingdom. We believe in loving on people around the world. And we believe in helping our investors pursue wealth through real estate investing, so they can increase their profits while being a force for God and the greater good.

For more information about how we can help you create generational wealth while impacting lives, go here to partner with us: InvestingWithPurpose.org/book

Motivate and Inspire Others!

Retail $19.95

Special Quantity Discounts

5-20 Books	$17.95
21-99 Books	$15.95
100-499 Books	$13.95
500-999 Books	$12.95
1,000+ Books	$11.95

Special Discount Pricing is subject to change.
Please contact us for final pricing options.

To Place an Order Contact
admin@integrityhg.com

Are You Looking for a Speaker for Your Next Faith-Based Event?

Are you looking for a down-to-earth Christian speaker who naturally connects with your audience?

Are you looking for a thought-provoking speaker who can show your congregation how to create generational wealth while simultaneously supporting their Christian values, so they can build the Kingdom?

Are you looking for a fun, passionate speaker who can show your flock how to make a significant impact in their local community as well as communities around the country and the world?

If you answered "YES" to any of the above questions, then look no further. Steven Libman has given hundreds of presentations around the country to Christian organizations like yours on topics like:

- Investing with Purpose: How to Align Your Investments with Your Worldview

- Growing in the Grace of Giving

- Investment Is Ownership, and Ownership Requires Stewardship

To Book Steven for Your Next Faith-Based Event, Send an Email to:

admin@integrityhg.com

Acknowledgements

I would like to extend my heartfelt gratitude to the following individuals who have played pivotal roles in the creation and journey of this book, *Investing with Purpose*.

To my esteemed business partner, Travis Cotter, and his wife, Stacey, thank you for your unwavering support, dedication, and partnership throughout our entrepreneurial and spiritual endeavors. I am grateful God has put us together.

To David and Jason Benham, mentors and guides in both spiritual and business matters, your wisdom, encouragement, and guidance have been invaluable. Your insights have shaped not only my approach to business but also my personal growth and faith journey. As Lloyd said, "Our pets' heads are falling off!"

I am deeply appreciative of all the mentors who have generously shared their knowledge and wisdom with me over the years. Your mentorship and wisdom saved me time, effort, and energy while guiding me through the twists and turns of entrepreneurship and life.

A heartfelt thank you to all our team members in the business, whose hard work, dedication, and passion have been the driving force behind our accomplishments. Your contributions are deeply appreciated and never go unnoticed. To quote Henry Ford, "Coming together is a beginning, staying together is progress, and working together is success."

Lastly, thank you to the investors who entrusted us with their hard-earned money, and thank you for your confidence and belief in our vision. Your support fuels our determination to make meaningful and impactful investments.

Together, we stand on the shoulders of giants, and I am immensely grateful for each and every one of you who has contributed to this journey.

With sincere appreciation,

Steven Libman